Brag, Worry, Wonder, Bet

Brag, Worry, Wonder, Bet

A Manager's Guide to Giving Feedback

Steve King

iUniverse, Inc.
Bloomington

Brag, Worry, Wonder, Bet
A Manager's Guide to Giving Feedback

iUniverse books may be ordered through booksellers or by contacting:

iUniverse
1663 Liberty Drive
Bloomington, IN 47403
www.iuniverse.com
1-800-Authors (1-800-288-4677)

ISBN: 978-1-4759-6874-3 (sc)
ISBN: 978-1-4759-6875-0 (ebk)

Library of Congress Control Number: 2013901470

Printed in the United States of America

iUniverse rev. date: 03/25/2013

Contents

To my mom and dad—who made many bets on me for which I will be forever grateful.

Why I Wrote This Book

1

I grew up with a lot of friends who were into music. Many of them played instruments, and all of us listened to music—constantly. There was always an

> Having a good feedback session is like playing a memorable song.

album on in the background, and certain favorite tracks were played over and over again. Grooves in the vinyl were literally worn out.

I noticed early on that the songs that really got my attention were those with some type of musical hook: a catchy little musical phrase that was memorable. I suppose this was one of the reasons we all liked the Beatles and the Stones—great hooks.

As I broadened my musical taste, I realize now the hooks were what drew me in. The beginning of Marvin Gaye's "What's Going On?" was my introduction to R&B. Paul Desmond's sweet alto at the beginning of "Take Five" was my introduction to jazz.

I liked those musical hooks!

When I became a teacher and eventually a corporate training guy, I realized pretty quickly that learning was like music. The best learning had these little hooks in it—something that drew the learner to the content being delivered or the skill being developed. There was something memorable that could be taken back to the workplace and used over and over again.

This book is about one of those hooks. I stumbled onto Brag, Worry, Wonder, Bet a lot like the way a musician might stumble onto a musical hook in the studio: I was just playing around.

I had been teaching a lot of management development programs. Topics like feedback and motivation and career coaching were always on the menu. And I had handy, various four-step processes and five simple principles for all of them. Good stuff? Yes, but it never seemed to connect like a great song. There was nothing memorable or catchy, just good, solid stuff.

Unsatisfied, I set out to find a better way to deliver the message of how to be a good manager. And after about a year of experimenting with various things, Brag, Worry, Wonder, Bet just appeared.

I started using it first as a personal management tool with those who worked for me and with me. Before long, I found many of these people using it as well. Later, I started introducing it in management programs as a simple framework for giving feedback. People leaving these sessions invariably cited BWWB as the one thing they most definitely were going to try back at the office. And when I had occasion to follow up with some of them, sure enough they were using it and seeing results.

This is the reason I have written this little book: to share with you this management hook. Enjoy.

Why Brag, Worry, Wonder, Bet? 2

Brag, Worry, Wonder, Bet is simply a dialogue starter, period. As you will see, there are many different kinds of dialogues or conversations that the technique can jump-start: feedback conversations, performance conversations, and career conversations.

And, as it turns out, Brag, Worry, Wonder, Bet is a pretty good framework for brainstorming with teams and even doing quick-and-dirty situation analysis.

But essentially it is nothing more than a dialogue starter.

Brag, Worry, Wonder, Bet reflects certain biases I have about work and the management of work, so I might as well put them right up front.

First, I prefer conversations over process. Now, don't get me wrong. We need process to manage performance, but if you want to improve performance and sustain that improvement, good conversations are what matter most.

> Brag, Worry, Wonder, Bet is a dialogue starter that helps center a potentially complex conversation.

Second, I like to keep things simple or, more accurately, to start simply. Conversations are always complex because people are complex, so to work through that complexity we need tools that keep us focused on what matters. I believe that is what BWWB does. It's a simple dialogue starter to ground or center a potentially complex conversation.

Finally, I like pedestrian words. I prefer plainspoken language to business speak or HR speak. Brag. Worry. Wonder. Bet. This is plain language that provokes some thought and is accessible to and understood by most people.

If you share these biases, I expect you will enjoy the book. If you do not share these biases, well, read on anyway. You might become convinced.

3

How to Brag, Worry, Wonder, Bet

Here is how I recommend you get started using BWWB.

Think about someone you would like to give feedback to. For our purposes here we'll call him Joe.

> "When I brag about you, I brag about . . ."

Finish the following four statements:

- When I brag about Joe, I brag about _____.
- When I worry about Joe, I worry about _____.
- When I wonder about Joe, I wonder about _____.
- If I bet on Joe, I would bet on _____.

Each of these statements is designed to address specific issues and opportunities. There's more detail further along in the book, but for now, here are the basics:

- Brags are about the things that are going well and that you want to reinforce.
- Worries are about the things that are not going well and you want to address, improve, and remedy.
- Wonders are curiosities about things that may impact performance, but you are not sure.
- Bets are predictions of what could happen in the future.

You could probably stop reading the book right here and have the gist of this framework. It is not particularly complicated. But whether you read on or not, try it out on someone. Pick someone first who you have more brags about than worries. That will make your first pass at this easier.

But if you want just a little detail and context, read on.

Why Bragging Is a Good Thing

4

When I was a kid, my parents were not very keen on people bragging about themselves. I have some pretty vivid memories of them

> Everyone likes to hear good things about their work.

chastising my sisters or me when we boasted about something we had done. I am sure they thought it was kind of unseemly and showed bad character.

But it did not go unnoticed by me that those very same parents would brag endlessly about the accomplishments of my sisters or me. A double standard? No, I don't think so. Bragging about someone else is not the same as bragging about oneself. And I have to admit, I liked it when my parents had good things to say about me. It could be embarrassing, but I liked it.

One of the reasons I liked hearing them brag is that it was, in a very real sense, a form of feedback to me. It clarified what they liked about me and what I did.

Of course, the same thing is true in the workplace. I have worked with executives, and I have worked with the folks on the shop floor, and they all have this in common: they like to hear good things about their work. They like to know what they are doing is appreciated. They like positive feedback.

This is why brag sits at the front of this framework. It establishes a positive tone for a conversation about performance or a feedback conversation and gives the person receiving the feedback a clear picture of how he or she is positively valued.

I played around with other words besides "brag." What I admire. What I value. But the bluntness and almost uninhibited nature of the word "brag" turned out to have a certain appeal. It seems that deep inside, most of us like to be bragged about—even at work.

> "Lisa, when I brag about you, I brag about how you nailed that project earlier this year. On time. Within budget. Client happy. It was great work."

Heck—who would not like this? Message sent and message clear.

5

Why Sharing Your Worries Is a Good Thing

For most of us the most difficult feedback to give someone is negative feedback. We have all become very savvy about how we position these kinds of conversations. We call them developmental feedback or constructive feedback. But honestly, no one is fooled when they hear, "I have some developmental feedback for you." They know what's coming. We know they know what's coming, and it is uncomfortable.

Unquestionably, this kind of feedback is crucial to all of us. We simply cannot learn and grow as people and as professionals without feedback that points out what we are doing wrong or what we are not doing that we should be doing. And it is a manager's responsibility to deliver this feedback.

I became convinced long ago that the secret to giving difficult feedback was to deliver the message with empathy and with a sense that you really are prepared to help someone get to a better place. Something like following a nice four-step process can help, but it is the personal touch that makes it really work.

The word that carried this sense of empathy and support turned out to be "worry."

Generally, when we worry about someone, it is because we care. And when we express this worry out loud, it is a gesture of caring.

While at first blush this may seem a bit too touchy-feely for the workplace, don't be fooled. It turns out to be just as powerful a dialogue tool at work as it is in your personal life.

> "Betty, I am worried you are struggling to get those reports done on time."

Message: I care about your struggle, and I want to help. This is a great jumping-off point for a productive dialogue. Hopefully, Betty's defenses are dampened a bit by the gesture of caring, and she is now more open to listening.

On one hand, I do not want to oversell "worry." It is not a magic word that makes all difficulty with these kinds of conversations go away. But it does tee up these kinds of conversations better than anything else I have tried.

On the other hand, I will suggest that the power of "worry" increases the more difficult the feedback is. Once I had to tell a person directly, "When I worry about you, I worry that people simply do not trust you." His jaw dropped. He got defensive. But I kept reiterating my "worry," and as the conversation progressed, his defenses came down, and we had the right conversation.

> Address poor performance both directly and with a commitment to help with improvement.

Perhaps more than the other three words in this dialogue framework, there is a serious integrity issue tied up with using the word "worry." As I suggested, worrying is about caring and being supportive. If you are really worried, it is a great word to use to start the important dialogue. If you really are not worried at all—if you frankly don't care and are not really supportive—then don't use the word.

Wonder and Curiosity in the Workplace

6

When I was first working out BWWB, it actually started as Brag, Worry, Bet. Wonder was not part of the deal. But as I played around with this framework, I realized

> Curiosity may have killed the cat, but it can be an asset to a manager.

that sometimes managers had something to say or ask that was neither a brag nor a worry. Instead, it was more of a curiosity. It might sound something like:

"I am curious whether your project's timeline could be moved up."

or

"I am curious what the rationale is for giving Paul the promotion you proposed."

Since "curious" is a little formal, I turned it into wonder.

"I wonder whether your project's timeline could be moved up."

or

"I wonder what the rationale is for giving Paul the promotion you proposed."

The hallmark of a wonder is its neutrality. Consider if the above statement had been,

"I wonder why you are promoting Paul when our compensation budget is so tight."

It would not have been neutral at all. It is a worry. And the person on the other end of this question knows the difference—instantly.

If you are worried about something, name it a worry and you will likely jump into a productive conversation about fixing that worry or concern.

If you are not worried, but only curious, name it a wonder and you will likely jump into a clarifying conversation and have your curiosity satisfied.

Oh, and by the way, if you have only worries and no wonders, then I suggest you reexamine your proclivity to see the glass half-empty. You will be happier for it, and so will those who work with you.

Making Bets on Other People

7

Betting is about the future. It is about guessing or predicting what will happen and having a stake in that outcome.

The most common use of the bet part of BWWB is as a means to kick off a career-development conversation in a provocative, attention-grabbing way.

Obviously, people are interested in their future, certainly the future of their careers. And they are generally also interested in what others think about their future possibilities and potential in the workplace.

So when a manager or colleague opens a conversation with one of these, the conversation shifts quickly into the what, why, when, and how mode—the meat of a good career conversation: "If I were to bet on you, Anne, I would bet . . .

> Managers should not avoid career conversations but initiate them.

you could do my job."

or

you could manage that project."

or

you could take on those new responsibilities."

Before someone verbalizes a bet about someone else, they need to be prepared to share the details. The person receiving the feedback will want to know why you would make the bet. And if the answer is, "Well, I don't know. I just think you would be good at it," the conversation is going to be less than satisfying.

If you are prepared and he or she is willing, a solid career conversation can be as satisfying as a good performance review or a great pay message.

The other nuance in framing the conversation in terms of a bet is that it suggests the bettor has a stake in the future of this person—that the bettor would put something on the line if he or she could. Like a worry, this frames the conversation in a slightly more intimate and authentic way. And that builds the trust necessary for a frank and honest career dialogue.

Finally, using the notion of betting on someone leads itself to the language of betting.

For example, "Anne, I think it is a sure bet that you could be my successor right now." Or "Anne, I really think it is a long shot at best for you to get that overseas assignment in the next year." Continued dialogue about either of these statements will probably bring to the surface various brags, worries, and wonders. And then the conversation becomes robust and meaningful and impactful—the goal of all BWWB moments.

Performance Conversations and Performance Management

8

Nearly all large organizations and many small firms have some type of performance-management process. These processes come in all sorts of shapes and sizes: formal, informal, long form, short form, 360 format, competencies models.

Some of them are quite good. Others are pretty bad.

There are six conversations that every manager needs to master.

I have found that the best performance-management processes have certain characteristics. They tend to be simple and easy to use. Documentation is part of the deal but not overbearingly so. The link between business goals, what someone must get done on the job, and the "what's in it for me" for that person are clearly apparent in the process. And it has an impact. It unquestionably contributes to the success of the business and the success of the person.

I do not believe that BWWB is a substitute for a good performance-management system. I think it is more of an enabler or a shorthand way to execute parts of such a system.

Here are six questions, written from the point of view of an employee, that I like to see answered by any good performance system:

1. What is expected of me?
2. What will I learn along the way?
3. How am I doing along the way?
4. How did I do in the end?
5. How are you going to reward me financially?
6. After this gig, what is next for me?

While BWWB can probably be twisted this way and that way to help address all of these questions, I particularly like it as a means for addressing:

- How am I doing along the way?
- How did I do in the end?
- After this gig, what is next for me?

These are essentially feedback issues, and BWWB is essentially a feedback framework.

Brags and worries give someone the conversational platform to suggest where things are going well and where things are not doing so well. Bets give managers the conversational platform to suggest what could be in an employee's job future. These conversations can tee up those parts of the performance-management process that can then migrate to the necessary formalities, like documentation.

9

Betting On Reaching Your Goals

Quite often, I have had someone participating in a session where I have presented BWWB suggest to me some unique or unusual twist on how to use these words. Here is one of my favorites:

The beginning of most performance-management processes is the goal-setting process. We all know the rules of the road here: SMART goals, stretch goals, developmental goals.

This manager took the idea of bet and applied it to working out goals with her staff. Sure bets became associated with goals that seemed easy to accomplish and therefore did not carry as great a reward. Push bets became associated with reasonable stretch goals and higher rewards. Long-shot bets were linked to goals that were too ambitious and were discouraged. And a trifecta became associated with

> A stretch goal by definition has risk. Taking on a stretch goal is a kind of bet that you expect will pay off.

interlocking goals that all needed to be achieved for a good year to be had.

This is a clever use of the framework. Personally, I am not so acquainted with the ins and outs of betting to take on this particular approach.

But it seemed to work for her, so more power to her.

Personal Brags, Worries, Wonders, Bets

One of the most common performance-assessment practices is to have the person being assessed do a self-evaluation in advance of the formal assessment conversation.

Generally, I like this practice. A little bit of reflection time, some of it taking stock, can be a good way to prepare for such an important conversation. Actually, it is wise to do this regardless of whether a formal assessment is on the horizon. I think the best performers I've known continuously examine their own performance and make the appropriate adjustments.

When assessing oneself prior to a formal discussion, it is sometimes awkward to use the organization's official assessment framework to do it. Typically these frameworks require selecting a rating:1, 2, 3, 4, 5 or A, B, C, D, E or exceeds, meets, does not meet.

In my experience people are comfortable making and even sharing qualitative assessments of themselves, but are skittish making quantitative assessments of themselves. And perhaps employees should be skittish with these frameworks, since often these quantitative ratings are linked to compensation ranges and performance thresholds.

> Asking someone to brag, worry, wonder, and bet about themselves taps the value of self-reflection.

Eventually, the approved forms will be filled out and ratings will be assigned. These are the manager's responsibilities. But prior to the formal assessment, consider asking for someone to do a BWWB analysis on themselves and to bring those reflections to the formal assessment conversation. These reflections can serve as a solid foundation for conversations about recent past performance and what lies ahead, which would leverage the open and nonthreatening nature of BWWB.

There will always be time for turning those reflections into the formal observations housed in a performance system. Opt for the good conversation first, then good documentation.

Brag, Worry, Wonder, Bet as Situation Analysis

The BWWB framework was initially developed for feedback to individuals. But as it turns out, it can also serve a purpose in group settings. In particular it is a great vehicle for doing a down-and-dirty situation analysis.

> Consider opening a meeting with a group Brag, Worry, Wonder, Bet.

To me, a situation analysis examines work and market environments for opportunities to exploit and issues to address. There are some excellent tools and processes for doing this type of analysis in a thorough and complete way. I would certainly recommend many of them.

But if a team wants to do a quick, informal situation analysis, BWWB can be a very effective format to do that.

Personally, I like to open up a team meeting with a kind of lightning round of BWWB. People just start tossing out various brags and so on.

I do not impose a lot of structure. For instance, I do not do a round of brags, followed by a round of worries, and so on. Instead, we let it flow wherever it flows, and then we debate vigorously.

We make a point of capturing thoughts on a flipchart or a whiteboard. More importantly, we actually use this list of observations. Sometimes, we adjust the meeting agenda to address something raised in the BWWB lightning round. Sometimes, we assign a task to someone to follow up on one or more of those observations.

Used this way, BWWB becomes a table setter for future work of promise and potential. It also reinforces the role of a team as an idea generator and priority setter.

12

Bragging, Worrying, Wondering, and Betting with a Large Group

Sometimes, managers hold meetings with more than just the workers who report directly to them: there might be 50 people or 100 people or even 150, depending on a manager's scope of responsibilities.

These meetings at a recent employer of mine were referred to as "infoshares."

Generally, I am a big fan of these types of meetings and see them as important components of a manager's communication strategy. They place the manager on the spot to deliver key messages and, ideally, to field questions about a variety of topics on the minds of employees. I think "going live" rather than staying entirely virtual through e-mails and blogs is a good thing.

However, I have trouble with most of the infoshares I've sat through as an employee because they are often one-way affairs. The manager has a lot to say and uses up most of the time available for the meeting saying it. When a Q&A is included in the agenda, it typically gets relegated to the end of the meeting when time is at a premium.

When I did infoshares, I viewed them as half mine and half those of the people attending the meeting. If the meeting was scheduled for an hour and a half, I viewed forty-five minutes as mine and forty-five minutes as theirs. That way I ensured that ideas and observations would flow both ways, not just one way.

Instead of a Q&A I did a group version of BWWB. I placed four flipcharts at the corners of the room. At the top of one I wrote in big letters "BRAG." On another, I wrote "WORRY," and so on. I then gave everyone five to ten minutes to jot down on a note card their personal BWWBs. If the group was large, I would ask them to huddle into groups of four or five and come up with some group BWWBs.

> Town halls and infoshares don't have to be a monologue—they can be two-way conversations.

Once the note-taking was done, I asked for volunteers to offer up their particular BWWBs. We would capture them on the appropriate flipchart. I would likely make comments about what was said. Others would as well. It invariably turned into a free exchange of thoughts. And it was fun.

The result? Participants felt they had been heard, and I had a wide range of information that I could use to help make improvements in performance, both mine and others'. I had brags worthy of recognition. I had worries needing attention. I had wonders needing clarification. I had bets worth consideration. All and all, it was a nice day's work for a manager—presuming some productive actions came of it.

One tactical point: nowadays, managers find themselves with employees spread all over the globe. This should not preclude creating two-way infoshares or using BWWB. It simply requires some creative use of technology, clear instructions, and being okay with the multitasking likely to be going on. If you have some learning or communications experts around, ask for their help. They probably know how to make this happen.

Public Bragging

13

One of the big surprises for me when I began using BWWB in group settings was how people tended to use their opportunity to brag.

I think I expected the brags to be kind of impersonal—things like compliments about the company's marketing campaign or its new benefits arrangements or exceeding market guidance.

And, while there are always some of these, most of the brags turned out to be quite personal and intimate. Someone would stand up in the back of the room and say something like, "I would like to brag about Lisa and her team. They really slam-dunked the roll-out of the employee survey. My business partners appreciated the ease of the implementation and are really looking forward to getting the data."

> For some, public recognition is the best recognition.

Of course, sprinkled throughout the room are Lisa and her team, now basking in the glow of some public recognition. It was not uncommon for a round of applause to follow the compliment. It was a great use of the brag.

And once one solid compliment about people in the room was expressed, it seemed to open the door for other brags to follow. In fact, it sometimes turned into a bit of a love fest with a lot of appreciation being shared.

I liked this very much. Most organizations fall short on the recognition front. Employees typically go far too long without expressions of appreciation, and public bragging successfully fills some of that void.

14

Remembering to Brag

Just as I sometimes find people who struggle to share their worries, there are those out there who have a hard time bragging about others as well. These are people who have a hard time for some reason giving others compliments or providing praise for good work.

I am not a shrink, so I am not qualified to suggest why certain people cannot seem to let a good comment pass their lips. But I have seen some really interesting approaches to helping people who want to get better at this actually brag more often. Here is my favorite:

I once worked with a senior executive who was a bit on the stuffy side but had a reputation for delivering regular and timely compliments to his extended staff, which was a large group. I wondered how someone inclined toward the conservative, who was somewhat quiet and a little austere, was such a good bragger.

> Some of us need "prompts" to remember to brag, sometimes something as simple as a few pennies in your pocket.

I got up the nerve to ask him how he came to be good at this. (I did not include the prologue about him being kind of a stiff.) His answer was surprising and inspiring.

Apparently he once was stingy with a compliment. He got some feedback from a mentor that he should change that. After pondering it with his wife one night, they concocted the following plan:

Each day, he would begin by putting five pennies in his right pocket. His task for the day was to deliver at least five compliments, recognitions, or brags during the course of the day. As he delivered each positive message, he would move one penny from his right pocket to his left pocket. His goal was to get all five pennies moved over by the end of day.

He said all was different after that. His goal orientation got leveraged into a bragging machine.

For those of you stingy with the compliment, find your "pennies in the pocket."

Wondering and Learning 15

What is the most profound learning experience you have ever had?

Even though I would love to hear someone say, "Well, the class I took from you, Steve King, is no doubt the most profound learning experience I ever had," I don't think I have ever heard that or will ever hear that.

Learning experts have debated for centuries how people learn, and I suspect that there is truth or half-truths in many of these theories supported by solid data and research.

One commonly accepted perspective is that learning begins with wonder.

There is a famous story that as a young man Albert Einstein wondered what it would be like to ride on a beam of light. Legend has it that this kind of wonderment led Einstein through the learning curve that brought him to the theory of relativity.

When you wonder about someone, you are expressing curiosity. As you express wonder in dialogue with a person, his or her responses and the conversation that ensues are learning moments—for you.

In this way the wonder part of BWWB is different. At first blush it is about your learning, not the other person's.

"When I wonder about you, I wonder about how you consistently bring projects in on time and within budget."

That statement is about your learning. Perhaps you are looking for some project-management tips to share with others or use yourself. Perhaps you want to learn something more formal about cost estimation or critical-path analysis.

> Our greatest learning sometimes starts by simply wondering about something or someone.

The point is you can leverage wonder as a means to learn from those you are giving feedback to. This dynamic between you and the other person can be a very healthy one.

Think of it. In the middle of a performance review, where you have already shared brags and worries, you can drift into a conversation in which the other person is now sharing and maybe teaching something to you. This momentary reversal of roles—the giver now the receiver—builds a sense of partnership between the two parties. It shows mutual respect. I think it can strengthen a relationship.

Can wonder also tee up learning for those receiving the feedback? Sure. Let's go back to the statement I made a moment ago:

"When I wonder about you, I wonder about how you consistently bring projects in on time and within budget."

If the response is, "I really don't know how I do it; it just sort of ends up that way," there is an opportunity to make more explicit what this person seems to be doing intuitively. You can explore what makes him or her successful. In that case he or she learns just as you learn. It's a win-win learning moment for both of you.

16

Bragging, Worrying, Wondering, and Betting in Your Personal Life

When I set out to develop what became BWWB, I was explicitly trying to find something that would succeed in the workplace. I was not trying to create something I could use in my personal life.

> Taking your work home has some risks, so proceed with caution.

But I must admit I have tried it out at home and in other parts of my life. For example, I was recently on the search committee for a new pastor at my church. I was assigned the task of doing reference checks. So I decided to use BWWB as my framework for those checks. It was pretty much the same formula:

> When you brag about Reverend So-and-So, what do you brag about?
>
> When you worry about Reverend So-and-So, what do you worry about?

And so on.

And it worked great.

On the other hand, using it with my wife at home got sort of mixed reviews. I guess it was a little like bringing office work home. More seriously, using workplace jargon might well demean a relationship rooted in more than a good performance conversation. The spirit of the framework probably has some value at home, but use the explicit framework at your own risk.

17

Customizing Your Very Own Brag, Worry, Wonder, Bet

When I present BWWB to various groups, there will inevitably be someone in the group who will take exception to one of the words. As you can tell if you have made it this far in the book, BWWB was the product of intuition, common sense, and trial and error—not serious research. So if a certain word does not quite fit your vocabulary or circumstances, I encourage you to find a better word. Or perhaps another way of saying it, find your own hook that kick-starts the right dialogues and drives the right conversations.

One worry I will share with you is how this framework works across various cultures.

> Make sure you find your unique voice as a manager, which means sometimes adjusting language to better fit the audience.

I have been lucky enough to have shared this framework with many people from many different cultural backgrounds. Whenever that happens, I try to grab that opportunity to ask anyone very different from me, "Do these words that I shared with you carry the same meaning in your culture?" Worry and wonder seem to hold up pretty well. Brag and bet, on the other hand, sometimes fail the test.

As we mentioned earlier, there is a bluntness and almost uninhibited nature about the word "brag" that some cultures just are not uncomfortable with. And the notion of "betting" does not play well with certain religious groups who find gambling offense and wrong.

My advice is to know your audience. If it is a culturally diverse audience, check in with them about your use of these words. And, if need be, make the necessary adjustment. But keep looking for the key result—great and productive conversations.

And good luck.

18

Example of an Abbreviated Brag-Worry-Wonder-Bet Conversation

The Manager: Hi, Gene, shall we get right to it?

Gene: Sure.

The Manager: You know the routine. I am going to talk about what I am currently bragging about when I brag about you, what I am currently worrying about, what I am wondering about, and what I would bet on if I were to bet on you. Have you been giving some thought to these as well?

Gene: Yes, and I have jotted some notes down I might want to share.

The Manager: Great. Well, let me get started. In the last quarter, the thing I have been really bragging about is the process improvement effort you lead. Those customers calling our ten service reps in the call center were waiting on hold far too long before someone was actually talking to them live. That was just unacceptable.

I love the approach you took to improving the situation. Your analysis of customer hold times was clear and spot on. It clarified the issue we wanted to address. And figuring out that more than 70 percent of those on hold had issues that could be easily addressed with a couple of telephonic questions without ever needing to talk to someone live was just brilliant.

Gene: It was a team effort. Everyone deserves credit.

The Manager: Sure they do. And they will get that credit. But right now I want to single out your efforts leading the team. You led the group from analysis of the problem to solution and implementation of a new telephonic system in eight weeks. We figured it would take at least twelve weeks. No more customer complaints about long waits.

You're feeling good about this too, right?

Gene: Yes, it was number one on my list of brags this quarter.

The Manager: Good. It should be number one. Let me jump over to one of my worries. Gene, when I worry about you, I worry about your forecasting of project implementation costs.

Gene: What do you mean?

The Manager: Let's stay on the call-center improvement process for a moment. The only thing that did not go well with that effort was your assessment of total cost of implementation.

Gene: I got the price tag for the telephonic system right! The quote I got is exactly what we paid for it.

The Manager: You're right, but the cost of the new system is not the whole cost of the project. It took about a hundred hours of IT's time to get the system up and running and in sync with our databases. And the training on the new system cost us about $20,000 in instructional-design fees. You did not account for these in your implementation costs.

Gene: But IT said it was no big deal.

The Manager: I suppose in the big scheme of things that IT's work on it was no big deal. But I want to make sure you understand what I am worried about here. If I were to bet on you, I would bet you have a great future with our company as a project manager of very large projects. We will talk about that in a moment. But good project managers understand that the cost of implementing something includes both external costs like the cost of the system and the cost of the instructional designers and the internal costs like the time of the IT staff.

Gene: But I am not sure I know exactly how to assess the internal costs. IT said it was no big deal, so I just took them at their word.

The Manager: Well, there are plenty of good, time-tested techniques for determining the cost of implementing a project. In fact, there is a project-management training course that will cover these techniques, plus a lot of other good stuff. I think we should sign you up.

You understand that my worry is not about something that can't be addressed, right?. It's just a skills gap that we can tackle with the class plus some coaching when you apply it. Understand?

Gene: Okay, I get it.

The Manager: So let's move on. When I wonder about you, Gene, I wonder if you would like to work in one of our overseas facilities in the next few years.

Gene: Really? I have thought about it, but I had no idea how people get selected for overseas assignments. It was on my list of wonders too. But I would have been too embarrassed to bring it up, I think.

The Manager: We can get into the ins and outs of expat assignments later. I just wanted to check in and see if you would be interested. Over the next three years, we expect to double our non-North American presence, and we will need folks to do two or three-year stints. We are just taking inventory of those interested at this point. I just wanted to take your temperature at this point in time.

Gene: Well, place me on the short list, and let me know when the possibility becomes real.

The Manager: Okay. Great. Now, let's back to that bet I mentioned earlier. If I were to bet on you, I would bet you would make a great project manager of large projects. You handle the smaller projects we throw at you really well, like the call-center process-improvement project we were talking about earlier.

Gene: Except the implementation costing.

The Manager: Yes, except the implementation costing. We'll take care of that. The bet I am focusing on here is the adjustment to much bigger projects. You have a great way of sizing up any change situation, organizing the required tasks to address the situation, and leading a group of people through those project tasks. My bet is that those skills will scale well in a big project. Practically a sure bet.

Gene: How big are we talking?

The Manager: Something with a budget north of $1 million and maybe twenty people on the team.

Gene: Man, that's twice the size of anything I have done so far. I would be worried I couldn't handle it.

The Manager: Why?

Gene: I don't know. Just seems like a pretty big jump.

The Manager: Remember a few years ago when you were asked to lead that small project moving warehouse sites? You probably thought that was too big but it turned out fine. Right?

Gene: Yes, I thought I would not be able to handle it, but it worked out pretty well.

The Manager: Sure it did. When I brag about you, one thing I often brag about is how much you have grown over the last few years and how you have stepped up to each new challenge. It's why I can make this bet.

Gene: So when might this happen?

The Manager: In the next year. Plenty of time to address the cost-forecasting issue we talked about. And keep this in mind: big projects increase your chances of an international assignment someday. Project management will be one of the key skill sets the powers that be will be looking for.

About the Author

Steve King is the director of executive education at the University of Wisconsin's School of Business and president of the SDK Group, which specializes in helping organizations find solutions to their talent management challenges.

Steve is the retired SVP of human resources for Hewitt Associates, a global human resources consulting and outsourcing firm. Steve has also served as the head of global talent management for Baxter Healthcare; faculty leader for the Bank of Montreal's Institute for Learning in Toronto; and vice president of management and professional development for Harris Bank in Chicago.

In Steve's early career years, he was an instructor and curriculum designer for the Wisconsin Vocational & Technical System.

Steve lives in Chicago with Karen, Adam, and Dodger the Dog and splits his time between Madison, Wisconsin, and the Chicago area.

Anyone interested in contacting Steve or ordering this book can go to Steve's website at www.bragworrywonderbet.com.

Made in the USA
Middletown, DE
08 September 2018